SAIBARA

SAIBARA

Translated by Tomer Inbar

Copyright 2025 Tomer Inbar
All rights reserved.
Library of Congress Control Number: 2024944997
ISBN 987-1-63405-075-3

Cover and text design: www.twentysixletters.com
Printed in Canada

Published by Chin Music Press
1501 Pike Place #329
Seattle, WA 98101
www.chinmusicpress.com

Horse Play/Horse Sense/
What a Horse is Not (of course it is)

> "She was celebrated for her fine singing and was especially skilled in Saibara. A great many aristocrats and their children, people with cosmopolitan tastes, came to study under her"*

What is it about *Saibara*?

Like many things they are lost. Displaced in time, place and language. But like many lost things they are stubbornly (subtly) resilient. Beautifully and insistently so. They echo not far from the surface, as reinvention, moving forward on the bones of what brings up the rear.

And yet, things here are not so simple (they seem to say). *Saibara* are: on their way to the palace, paying tribute to an ancestor or the new year, urging the horses on, illegal gambling, teasing the upper class, a shy glance, smiling at (turning away from) a lover, the morning after, a line on the pages of *Genji*, this rhythm or that rhythm indistinguishable to my ears on YouTube (faithful to what was but one moment in their history), heard in the basement of a bookstore in Brooklyn in February or late afternoon in Portland in spring.

I came to *Saibara* looking for something else. Focused on how language gets made and then re-made at different times and for different purposes, *Saibara* were the gateway to the real target: the early Japanese books of myth (*Kojiki*) and poetry (*Man'yōshū*). A manageable first step. *Saibara* are (potentially and perhaps originally) folk songs—technically: urge/horse/song—appropriated as tradition to become aristocratic, courtly, stylized and performed/performative. They appear at court, are quoted/referenced in the Japanese classics and are critically studied (sporadically) throughout Japanese literary history,

---

* *Sandai Jitsuroku* first year of the Engi era/901 CE, from an entry dated the 23rd day of the 10th month of Jogan I (859 CE).

though not centrally and never canonized the way other early works were.

Neither fish nor fowl: *Saibara* are song and dance and language winking and low and vulgar and bawdy and base and sexual, and cosmopolitan and hiding. But most of all (to me) they are poetry.

I love the possibilities inherent in the language and form of Japanese poetry. The movement and internal dialogue. The space and motion. The way things take off in different directions and simultaneously: multi-jurisdictional. Though, I get that I read a lot into what I take out of it. I came to Japanese (language and poetry) as a young writer working through my own taste and style. Influenced by William Carlos Williams and formatively taught (or more accurately, "engaged with") by Robert Creeley (thanks to others as well, of course), I was thinking at the time about the quality of moment as momentum. And how things get defined or define themselves (the concept/variation on theme of "all things in itself, say it with things" was an early organizing principle) and how to do all that with poetry.

The structure of early Japanese writing systems/mechanisms drew me in as part of this exploration. I was attracted to the shift in the Japanese language from oral to written and how the initial use of Chinese characters in a clunky writing system known as *man'yōgana*—from its use in the *Man'yōshū*—was a step to the current hybrid system of syllaberry (*kana*) + character (*kanji*) and what that all meant for writing poetry. And that gets us back to *Saibara*, written in *man'yogana*, which for a stylized song/dance genre was probably their least relevant "in the moment" aspect, unless you care about them as poetry. And I did (and still do).

Although untangling the formal language was the initial attraction, in the end I stayed for the poetry. These translations reflect that approach. They are also necessarily of my own style and rendering, although I have tried to be as faithful as possible to a language that has been puzzled over and constructed/reconstructed over the past 800 plus years (so...faithful is definitely a relative, best-efforts concept).

In the end (and for a long time now) I find/have found *Saibara* magical as poetry. Each song/poem contains something knowing and fresh and moves in its own sly and emphatic way. They are light and oddly contemporary, filled with moments of awareness, engagement, mischief, knowing nods, and insight.

Enjoy.

Ritsu

(#1) my horse)

giddy-up

my horse

go out
quickly

& cross

Matsuchiyama

    ahare

Matsuchiyama

    hare

Matsuchiyama

where
someone

may be
waiting

go out quickly

    ahare

go out quickly
to see

(her)

(#2) *Sawada* river)

Sawada river

my sleeves
barely

reach it

> ***ya***

& though it is
shallow

> ***hare***

& though it is
shallow

attendants

from

the palace
at *Kuni*

> ***ya***

cross it

with

a lofty
bridge

ahare

how good it
must be

to cross

on that lofty
bridge

(#3) Takasago)

at *Takasago*

among the sand

at *Takasago*

on its ridge

stand

white
pearl

precious
camellia

precious
willow

wanting them

is how
I want you

it is you
I want

a cord white
& softened

a cord of dye

to hang
my robe

precious willow

why was it

> *sa*

why was it

why was it

had my heart not
been impatient

then the lily

> *sa*

then the lily

blooming in
the morning

that first
flower

opened

the one
I had

met

> *sa*

the lily

(it)

would
have
been

(#4) summer spinning)

(hey)

with
seven skeins
of summer
white
thread
I have

spun

    sa

I will weave

a robe

for you to wear

leave your wife

    yo

you speak

such nonsense

the things you say

woman

can your linen robe

approach my wife's

well-made sleeves

comfortable

to wear

fine shoulders

how the collar
fits with ease

would yours
fit like this

could you
weave one

like this

for me to wear

(#5) *Nuki* river)

the shoals of
Nuki river

are a soft
pillow

my arms

fold
into

softly

sleeping

not one
night

away

from your
parents

away

from your
parents

you

are more
beautiful

if that is so

I will go

to the market
at *Yawagi*

& buy shoes

if you

buy
shoes

buy

strong
cloth sandals

low & narrow

put them

on your feet

put on
your skirt

&

start off
on the road

to *Miyaji*

(#6) an *Azuma* hut)

(as from)

an *Azuma* hut

(as from)

a *Ma* hut

where rain
falls

from

eaves &
thatch
unkempt

I stand wet
by the gate

open

the door
to this villa

were this

a villa

with latch
or lock

I would

certainly

have bolted it

(just)

push it open

come in

I am already
yours

(#6) an *Azuma* hut)

(as from)

an *Azuma* hut

(as from)

a *Ma* hut

where rain
falls

from

eaves &
thatch
unkempt

I stand wet
by the gate

open

the door
to this villa

were this

a villa

with latch
or lock

I would

certainly

have bolted it

(just)

push it open

come in

I am already
yours

(#7) the running spring)

by the running
spring

gather cuttings

of

small reeds

&

from them
make

a cocoon

from which
to spin

thread

(#8) the *Asuka* spring)

by the *Asuka* spring

where we

should rest

    ya

    oke

its shade is

pleasant

drinking
water

cool

&

grass

good

for grazing

(#9) a young willow)

the strands of
a green
willow

twist

as a string
of thread

    ya

    oke ya

as the bush
warbler

    oke ya

as the hat

the bush
warbler

weaves

    oke ya

is a hat

of plum
blossoms

    ya

(#10) the sea at *Ise*

on the virgin
beaches

of the sea
at *Ise*

as the tide
recedes

I will pick
Nanoriso

I will gather
shell(fi)s(h)

I will gather
jewels

(#11) growing in the garden)

the *Kara Nazuna*

growing

in the garden

is a good
plant

hare

as they
spread

themselves

into
dangling
baskets

of the palace
attendants

(#12) by the gate of my house)

by the gate of
my house

by the gate of
my house

the hem of my skirt is wet
the hem of my slip is wet

picking plants
from
morning

picking plants
from
evening

picking plants
from
morning

picking plants
from
morning

picking plants
from
evening

if you want to know my name

in the garden of

in the garden of

in the garden of

in the garden of

the chief

of

the region

of

Ayame

call(s) me

his cherished
daughter

call(s) me

his younger
daughter

(#13) the gate of my house)

the man

walking
back & forth

leisurely

before the gate

of my house

has not come
with any intentions

he seems
to have

come

only

with

intentions

the man without
intentions

walking back
& forth

leisurely

with intentions only

has he come

with intentions only
has he come

(#14) the grand boulevard)

following along the
grand boulevard

as I climb
with it

the flowers of a
young willow (do)

the flowers of a
young willow (do)

at the sight of
young willows

draped &
billowing

aren't they

luxuriant
now

they are

luxuriant
now

       ya

(#15) large leaves of parsley)

large leaves

of parsley

are forbidden

in the country

(though even)

small leaves

are delicious

when

boiled

this is how it is:

first a board

from the wood
of a *Sandah* tree

a board from *Yushi*
wood made

a tube ridden hollow

bitten by worms

dice from a
rhino's horn

flat dice
throw
the dice

sides

slightly
raised

carved in sections

gold trims
a wooden board

turn over

five
&
six

the dice show
one & six

        ya

the dice show
four & three

        ya

(#16) *Asamuzu*)

the sounds of

the bridge
at *Asamuzu*

pounding
pounding

(with)

falling rain

my body
grown old

who

is this matchmaker

suggesting
(her)
description

in a letter
brought

perhaps

(or)

on a visit
come

sakimudachiya

(#16) Asamuzu)

the sounds of the bridge
at *Asamuzu*

pounding
pounding

with fallen rain

with my body
grown old

who will answer
this matchmaker

describe themselves
in a letter

perhaps

come visit

    ya

    sakimudachiya

(#17) a comb for (her) hair)

seventeen combs

for (her)
hair

ten & seven
there were

until an officer
from Takeku

who took

from those combs
the morning
he came

then took again
at evening
the same

he took from those combs
& now there are none

the combs from her hair
are none

(#18) a baby hawk)

please

grant me
a baby hawk

I'd put it on
my hand

& send it

to hunt

the quail

that fly

around

the chestnut
trees

growing

along the fields of
Awazu

      sakimudachiya

(#19) the *Ōmi* road)

do not pull
so quickly

the bamboo
grass

& butterbur

by the road where
we meet

I am with child

will you wait
for me

to become thin

(among)

the bamboo
grass

& butterbur

    sakimudachiya

(#20) the mouth of the road)

pleasant wind

tell my parents

I am here

at the

government

office

of *Takefu*

here

at the mouth of

the road

sakimudachiya

(#21) a change of clothes)

let us (ex)change

our

robes

    sakimudachiya

the one I wear

has been

rubbed

with

blossoms

of bush clover

from

grass plains

from fields of
bamboo

grass

    sakimudachiya

(#22) what should I do)

what

should I do

should I do

it

precious mallard

if I go out

though my
parents

scold me

for playing

around

I haven't
taken

an evening

lover

(yet)

sakimudachiya

(#23) the bird has sung)

The bird has sung

chokasa

& *Sakuramaru*
took his thing

(he took his thing)
& pushed it in

(he pushed it in)
& came again

(he came again)
& stayed until

(he stayed until)
her belly was filled

until with child
It filled

(#24) the old mice)

at *Nishidera*

the old mice do

the young mice

do chew

on the
robes

they chew

on (his) garments
chew too

chew on (his)
garments

they do

& should we tell
the priest

tell the priest

& should we tell
the priest

tell the priest

(#25) between her legs the names)

between her legs

the names

for it

how

do you

say it

between her legs

the names

for it

how

do you

say it

tsuratari
kyokuno
tamoro

tsuratari
kyokuno
tamoro

Ryo

(#26 how magnificent)

how magnificent

today's
magnificence

> *ya*

of old as well

> *hare*

of old as well

was it this way

> *ya*

the magnificence

of today

> *ahare*

how good it is

the magnificence

of today

(#27 a new year)

at the start

of a new year

beginning

    ya

this is certainly

how

    hare

this is certainly

how

I will serve

    ya

until many

generations

pass

    ahare

how good

it will be

until many

generations

pass

(#28) a plum branch)

on a plum branch

a warbler

there

is

    ya

passing into spring

    hare

passing into spring

though

it is crying

still

    ya

snow

continues

falling

    hare

how good it is

snow

continues

falling

(#29) Sakura(man))

(hey) Sakura(man)

stop that boat

I have
island
fields
ten *chō*
in all

I'll see them
then
return
here

    ya

      soyoya

tomorrow

I'll
return
here

      soyoya

it's all talk

when you say

tomorrow

it will be

while far
away

my husband
has left
a wife
behind

tomorrow
certainly (he)
will not
come

    ya
    soyoya

    sa

tomorrow
certainly (he)
will not
come

    ya
    soyoya

(#30) a reed fence)

(over) the reed fence

(through)

the *Ma* fence

part the *Ma* fence

jump

cross
over

on my back

cross
over

& who
jumps
across

& who
& who

maligns me

has told my
parents
on me

in this house
creaking

the youngest
daughter

of this house

makes trouble for me

has told my
parents
on me

it is not so

let the gods of
let the gods of

heaven & earth

bear witness
to the truth

I did not tell
my parents

nor malign
you

like a root of sedge

to the
cold
cold

words

said

I listen

must I listen
to them

(#31) Yamashiro)

in *Yamashiro*

(near Koma)

a melon grower

> **na**
>
> **nayoya**
> **raishinaya**
> **saishinaya**

a melon grower
a melon grower

> **hare**

a melon grower
has his eye
on me

they say

what should I do

> **na**
>
> **nayoya**
> **raishinaya**
>
> **ya**
>
> **saishinaya**

what should I do
what should I do

hare

what should I do

would it be so bad

(with him)

until the melons ripen

      **ya
raishinaya
saishinaya**

'til the melons ripen

until the melons ripen

(#32) smelting iron)

smelting iron

(in) the inner
mountains
of *Kibi*

a sash

around
them

> **nayoya**
> **raishinaya**
> **saishinaya**

making

a sash

around
them

making a sash

around
them

> **hare**

as it makes
a sash

around
them

clear sound

narrow

valley

stream

    ya
    raishinaya
    saishinaya

its clear
sound

the clarity
of
its sound

(#33) the region of *Ki*)

on the white beaches of *Ki*

on its pure white
beaches

hey (sea)gull

(you)

there

landed

    hare

bring
those
pearls

as the wind

certainly
blowing

as those ripples

certainly
rising

as the depths

are murky

hare

those pearls

cannot
be seen

(#34) Kazuragi)

it is in front of
the temple at
Kazuragi

    ya

it is to the west of
the temple at
Toyora

    ya

in a well spring

the leaves
of a lotus
tree

shimmer

like white
jewels

    ya

shimmer

like pure
white
jewels

    ya

ooshitodo
oshitodo

as this

is

so

the country
will certainly
flourish

ya

our houses
will certainly
prosper

ya

ooshitodo
toshitondo

ooshitondo
toshitondo

(#35) *Take* river)

(it is)
at the edge of
the bridge of
Take river

    ya

(it is)
at the edge
of the bridge

    ya

in that flower
garden

    hare

in that flower
garden

let me run free

    ya

let me run free

    ya

together
young
girls
with
me

(#36) Kawaguchi)

at *Kawaguchi*

its gateway is
gaps &
hedges

    ya

the gateway has
gaps in the
hedges

    ya

& though they watch it

    hare

& though they watch it

(I) go out from it
to sleep (with you)

    ya

(I) go out from it
to sleep (with you)

    ya

the gaps
in the hedge
of the gateway

(#37) this villa)

this villa

truly is
truly is

prosperous

with braids of three branches

    ahare

with braids of three branches

    hare

with braids of three branches

thatch three layers

thatch four layers

among which

a villa is built

    ya

among which

a villa is built

    ya

(#38) to the west of this villa)

to the west of this villa

the west storehouse

hedge

on a spring day

even

ahare

on a spring day

even

hare

on a spring day

even

though
I walk

even

though
I walk

I do not exhaust it

west storehouse hedge

    ya

west storehouse hedge

(#39) deep within this villa)

deep within this villa

deep within

where

an old woman

brews

sake

    ahare

an old woman

there

    hare

the old woman

there

seems to

she seems to

love me

is it the voice
of the *sake*

it is the voice
of the *sake*

        ya

(#40) Takayama)

to *Takayama*

a hawk

a hawk
I will let loose

with no way

to coax it

back

hare

with no way

to coax it

back

if I do

if I do it

then

is it my lover
who
I meet

is it my lover
who
I meet

(#41) Mimasaka)

(in) *Mimasaka*

    ya

(in) *Sarayama*
Kume
(they)

will never
ever

    nayoya

will never
ever

    nayoya

will never
ever

give my name
give my name
away

until many generations
pass

    ya

until many generations
pass

    ya

(#42) a field of wisteria growing)

a field of wisteria growing

(is) shaped as

(is) shaped as
a plain

lay stake(s)
around
it
    nayoya

lay stake(s)
around
it
    nayoya

lay stake(s)
around

cleanse &
celebrate

it

(is) evident (that)

the time must be fitting

    ya

the time must be fitting

    ya

(#43) my beloved & me)

with my
beloved

with me

on *Irusa* mountain

the mountain
araragi

in my hand(s)

take them

touch them

    ya

her scent is
exceptional

    ya

dangerously
exceptional

    ya

(#44) in pale shades of green)

in pale shades of green

in deep
light

blue

dyed & streaming
as far as you can see

those jewels
shining

shining
down

in the new capital

along *Suzuga*
avenue

(those)
willows trailing

or by the field shacks

in the gardens

autumn clover
nadeshiko
hollyhock

(those)
willows trailing

(#45) a piebald horse)

should a piebald
horse
run off

catch &
tether it

should a navy
horse
run off

catch &
tether it

(like) feather arrows
flying

(like) feather arrows
flying

Saseko's great-grandkid

is such
a mensch

such a talent and a mensch

Saseko's

great-grandkid

is

(#46) the gate of my beloved)

the gate of his beloved (is)
the gate her beloved

walking past
cannot pass
by

    ya

& if I walk by

let a sudden rain fall

my sleeves
raised
against it

my sleeves
raised
against it
little cuckoo

shelter (me)

from
the rain

an umbrella to
shelter me

I am coming in
for shelter

little cuckoo

(#47) Mushiroda)

in *Mushiroda*
in *Mushiroda*

by the *Itsunuki* river

  ya

for the cranes
living
there

for the cranes
living
there

  ya

for the cranes
living
there

a thousand years
I wish

frolicking
overhead

a thousand years
I wish

frolicking
overhead

(#48) Ohomiya)

to the west of
Ohomiya

on a small
road

where

the *Ayame*
grows
wild

    sa

an *Ayame*
gives
birth

to a child

    tarari
    yarin
    tanari

(#49) *Agemaki*)

(hey) *Agemaki*
child

    ya
    tōtō

though
two arm's
lengths

    ya
    tōtō

apart

we were
lying

tossing
we
turned

    tōtō

towards
each
other
we
turned

    tōtō

(#50) with trees luxuriant)

with trees luxuriant

with trees luxuriant

the middle
mountains

of *Kibi*

since long ago

from long ago
from long ago

since long ago

that their name
has not
grown
old

is because of this
age

is because of this
day

(#51 *Minoyama*)

they grow thickly
on *Minoyama*

the jeweled
oak do

& appear

at a
banquet

where I am
too

with delight

I meet them
there

  ya

with delight

I meet them
there

  ya

(#52) Mayutojime)

take (the horse)

fodder

& feed
it

mayutojime

mayutojime

mayutojime

mayutojime

mayutojime

mayutojime

mayutojime

(#53) drink some *sake*)

drink some *sake*

get drunk

drinking
some

    tafutokoriso

& certainly

come

for a visit

staggering
stumbling

come for a visit

come for a visit

come for a visit

(#54) among the paddies)

among the paddies
in a well spring

are *tanagi*
shining

pick them
pick them

my little girl

my tiny
little
girl

      tatarirari

among
the paddies

my tiny
little
girl

(#55) a frog with no strength)

(you are)

a frog with no
strength

a frog with no
strength

an earthworm
with no
bones

an earthworm
with no
bones

(#56) the sea at *Namba*)

the sea at *Namba*

the sea at *Namba*

paddle on

up (stream)

small
boat

big
boat

until the *Tsukushi*
offing

now a little
more

up (stream)

until *Yamazaki*

(#57) Suzuka river)

it is the *Suzuka* river

eighty rapids

swiftly

flowing

all people

praise

its effects

obviously

it is

fitting

now

yes

it is

fitting

now

(#58) Ishikawa)

in *Ishikawa*

by a *Koma*
man

my sash was taken

oh

how I
regret
it

& which
& which

sash
was it

oh

(the) light blue
sash

slit

on the inside

> **kayaruka**
> **ayaru**

did he
slip it
inside

(#59) the deep mountains)

in the deep
mountains

old man

are you
cutting
trees

& trees

will you
carve

beautiful trees

will you
carve
them

old man
carving
trees

(#60) the deep (deep) mountains)

in the deep (deep)
mountains

float
trees

(downstream)

old man of
Sakaki

& what of the trees

& what of the trees

the beautiful
trees

will you
carve
them

will you
carve
the trees

old man
carving
trees

(#61) my house)

in my house

even
the
curtains

hang

(to the floor)

let a great lord
come

take him

as a son-in-law

what would
be good

to entertain

him

with

abalone
sadawo
sea urchin

would be good

abalone
sadawo
sea urchin

would be good

www.ingramcontent.com/pod-product-compliance
Lightning Source LLC
Chambersburg PA
CBHW061810070526
44586CB00024B/2787